Doug Leko

Stashtastic!

12 Patterns for Fat-Quarter Quilts

Martingale
Create with Confidence

Dedication

To my mother, Elaine Leko. Without you I would never have learned this wonderful art. You've always encouraged me to do what I wanted and supported me endlessly along the way. I'll always be thankful for the many things you taught, showed, and shared with me.

Stashtastic! 12 Patterns for Fat-Quarter Quilts
© 2017 by Doug Leko

Martingale®
19021 120th Ave. NE, Ste. 102
Bothell, WA 98011-9511 USA
ShopMartingale.com

Printed in China
22 21 20 19 18 17   8 7 6 5 4 3 2 1

Library of Congress Cataloging-in-Publication Data
is available upon request.

ISBN: 978-1-60468-869-6

MISSION STATEMENT

We empower makers who use fabric and yarn to make life more enjoyable.

CREDITS

PUBLISHER AND
CHIEF VISIONARY OFFICER
Jennifer Erbe Keltner

CONTENT DIRECTOR
Karen Costello Soltys

MANAGING EDITOR
Tina Cook

ACQUISITIONS EDITOR
Karen M. Burns

TECHNICAL EDITOR
Nancy Mahoney

COPY EDITOR
Sheila Chapman Ryan

DESIGN MANAGER
Adrienne Smitke

COVER AND
INTERIOR DESIGNER
Regina Girard

PHOTOGRAPHER
Brent Kane

ILLUSTRATOR
Christine Erikson

SPECIAL THANKS
Thanks to Susanne Hartsock and Jack and Judy Cornwall of Woodinville, Washington, for allowing us to photograph this book at their homes.

Contents

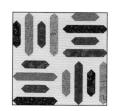

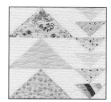
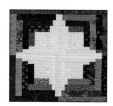

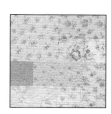
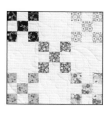

There's more online: Pieced Backings

Go to ShopMartingale.com/FQbackings to download free pieced backing options.

Introduction

When I think of quiltmaking, I think of colors. I've always loved playing with color as well as admiring how other quilters work with color. I'm amazed by the way colors play together and how they stand on their own. When I see a colorful quilt made with many fabrics, either from the same color family or completely scrappy, I am amazed. As I think of how to achieve this look, the answer is simple—use fat quarters!

Fat quarters, in my opinion, are the best size of precut fabric you can get. I know that many quilters agree. I find that the fat quarter is the one cut of fabric almost all quilters have in their stashes. It makes sense. At 18" x 21", a fat quarter is usually large enough to include the entire design of a print or to show the whole repeat. I love playing with fat quarters when designing, shuffling them around and swapping them for other pieces to see which fabric I like best. There are so many things you can create with them! When you want a great collection of prints, colors, and styles, fat quarters are the most economical way to achieve that desire.

When I started designing the quilts for this book, I knew I wanted them each to stand on their own, both in design and fabrics used. Each design in this book is shown in two colorways to get your creative juices flowing. I love the way a change of fabric can make a pattern look very different—and offer different styles for different tastes. If you decide to use scraps from your stash or start with more fat quarters than called for, please note that you'll still need to cut the total number of pieces listed in parentheses in the cutting list.

I love each and every one of the quilts in this book, and I hope you will too. Whether you're using hundreds of fabrics or a limited palette to create these versatile designs, *your* version will look great. So dive into your collection of fat quarters, enjoy yourself, and make your quilts your own!

- Doug -

English Knot

While this quilt appears complicated, it actually goes together easily. Pair two different fabrics in each block to ensure that all of the block combinations are unique.

Materials

Yardage is based on 42"-wide fabric. Fat quarters measure 18" × 21".

5¼ yards of gray print for blocks, sashing, and setting triangles

18 fat quarters of assorted prints for blocks and binding

6 yards of fabric for backing

77" × 99" piece of batting

Cutting

All measurements include ¼"-wide seam allowances.

From the gray print, cut:

3 strips, 22" × 42"; crosscut into:
- ◊ 3 squares, 22" × 22"; cut into quarters diagonally to yield 12 side triangles (2 will be extra)
- ◊ 2 squares, 11½" × 11½"; cut in half diagonally to yield 4 corner triangles

3 strips, 14½" × 42"; crosscut into 48 rectangles, 2½" × 14½"

5 strips, 4½" × 42"; crosscut into:
- ◊ 72 rectangles, 2½" × 4½"
- ◊ 4 squares, 4½" × 4½". Cut into quarters diagonally to yield 16 sashing triangles (2 will be extra).

15 strips, 2½" × 42"; crosscut into 233 squares, 2½" × 2½"

From *each* print fat quarter, cut:

2 strips, 4½" × 21"; crosscut into 12 rectangles, 2½" × 4½" (216 total)

2 strips, 2½" × 21"; crosscut into 13 squares, 2½" × 2½" (234 total)

1 strip, 2¼" × 21" (18 total)

FINISHED QUILT: 68⅜" × 91" ～ **FINISHED BLOCK: 14" × 14"**
Pieced by Doug Leko and Janet Moser; quilted by Sandy Pluff

Making the Blocks

For each block, choose eight rectangles and five squares from one print and label them as print A. Choose four rectangles and eight squares from a contrasting print and label them as print B. Instructions are for making one block. Repeat the steps to make a total of 18 blocks. Press all seam allowances as indicated by the arrows.

1 Draw a line from corner to corner on the wrong side of eight gray 2½" squares. Place a marked square on one end of a print A rectangle, right sides together. Stitch on the drawn line. Trim away the excess corner fabric, leaving a ¼" seam allowance. The unit should measure 2½" × 4½". Make four units.

Make 4 units,
2½" × 4½".

2 Place a marked gray square on one end of a print B rectangle, right sides together. Stitch on the drawn line. Trim away the excess corner fabric, leaving a ¼" seam allowance. The unit should measure 2½" × 4½". Make four units.

Make 4 units,
2½" × 4½".

3 Sew a gray 2½" square to a print B square to make a two-square unit. The unit should measure 2½" × 4½". Make four units.

Make 4 units,
2½" × 4½".

4 Join the units from steps 1 and 3 to make a 4½" square. Make four units.

Make 4 units,
4½" × 4½".

5 Sew a print A rectangle to the left side of a step 4 unit. The unit should measure 4½" × 6½". Make four units.

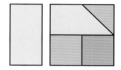 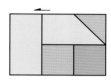

Make 4 units,
4½" × 6½".

6 Sew a print A square to one end of a step 2 unit to make a unit that measures 2½" × 6½". Make four units.

 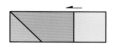

Make 4 units,
2½" × 6½".

7 Sew the step 6 units to the bottom of the step 5 units to make four quadrants measuring 6½" square.

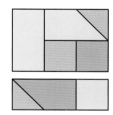 

Make 4 quadrants,
6½" × 6½".

8 Sew a print B square to one end of a gray 2½" × 4½" rectangle to make a 2½" × 6½" unit. Make four units.

Make 4 units,
2½" × 6½".

9 Lay out the quadrants, step 8 units, and one print A square in three rows as shown. Sew the pieces together into rows. Join the rows to complete one block. The block should measure 14½" square, including the seam allowances. Make a total of 18 blocks.

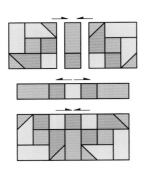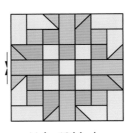

Make 18 blocks,
14½" × 14½".

Assembling the Quilt Top

1 Lay out the blocks, gray 2½" × 14½" rectangles, gray 2½" squares, and gray side and corner triangles in diagonal rows as shown in the quilt assembly diagram above right. Sew the pieces together into rows.

2 Join the rows to complete the quilt top, adding the corner triangles last. The setting triangles are cut slightly oversized for easier cutting and piecing. Trim and square up the quilt top,

making sure to leave ¼" beyond the points of the sashing for the seam allowance.

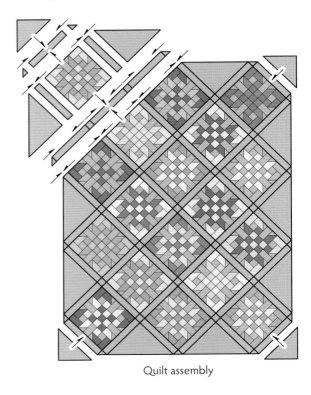

Quilt assembly

3 Stitch around the perimeter of the quilt top, ⅛" from the outer edges, to lock the seams in place.

Finishing

For more details on any of the following steps, go to ShopMartingale.com/HowtoQuilt for free downloadable information.

1 Layer the quilt top with batting and backing. Baste the layers together.

2 Hand or machine quilt. The quilt shown is quilted with an overall swirl design. Trim the batting and backing so the edges are even with the quilt top.

3 Use the assorted print 2¼"-wide strips to make scrappy binding, and then attach it to the quilt.

Alternate Colorway

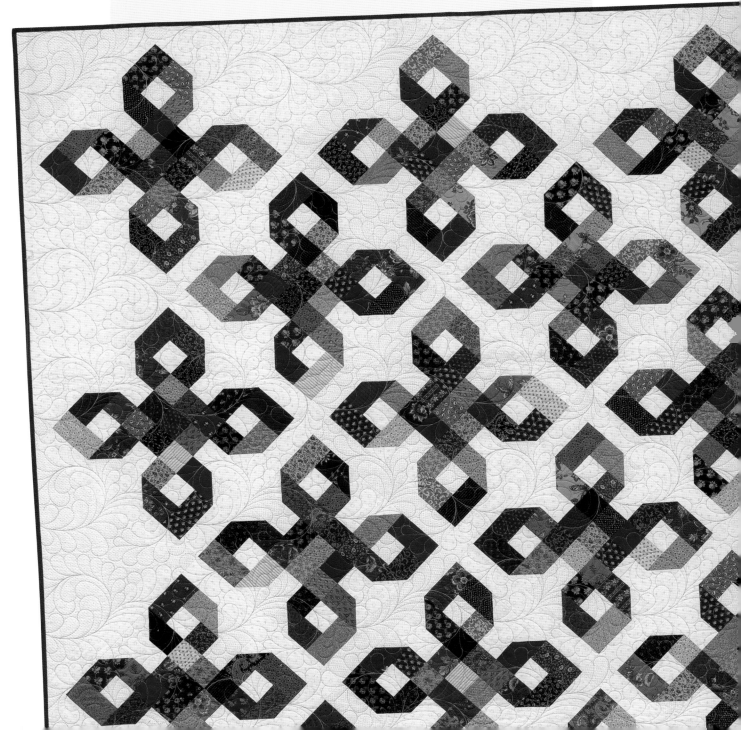

Because this version of English Knot is truly scrappy, it isn't necessary to pair your fabrics as instructed in "Making the Blocks" on page 9. For the blocks, you'll need 3⅛ yards of assorted prints or scraps, cut into a total of 216 rectangles, 2½" × 4½", and 234 squares, 2½" × 2½". For single-fabric binding, you'll need ⅝ yard of fabric cut into 9 strips, 2¼" × 42".

Pieced by Doug Leko and Janet Moser; quilted by Steve and Deb Palmer

Which Direction?

What an excellent opportunity to use your favorite fat quarters! The different sizes of each piece in the blocks and the variety of prints used will add to the overall design. It will make a great graduation gift for that special grandchild or friend.

Materials

Yardage is based on 42"-wide fabric. Fat quarters measure 18" × 21".

2⅞ yards of cream print for blocks, sashing, and border

8 fat quarters of assorted prints for blocks

½ yard of dark print for binding

3⅝ yards of fabric for backing

58" × 70" piece of batting

Cutting

All measurements include ¼"-wide seam allowances.

From the cream print, cut:

4 strips, 11½" × 42"; crosscut into
   91 rectangles, 1½" × 11½"

11 strips, 2½" × 42"; crosscut *5 of the strips* into
   80 squares, 2½" × 2½"

13 strips, 1½" × 42"; crosscut into
   332 squares, 1½" × 1½"

From *each* print fat quarter, cut:

5 strips, 2½" × 21"; crosscut into:
   ◇ 5 rectangles, 2½" × 11½" (40 total)
   ◇ 5 rectangles, 2½" × 7½" (40 total)

From the dark print, cut:

6 strips, 2¼" × 42"

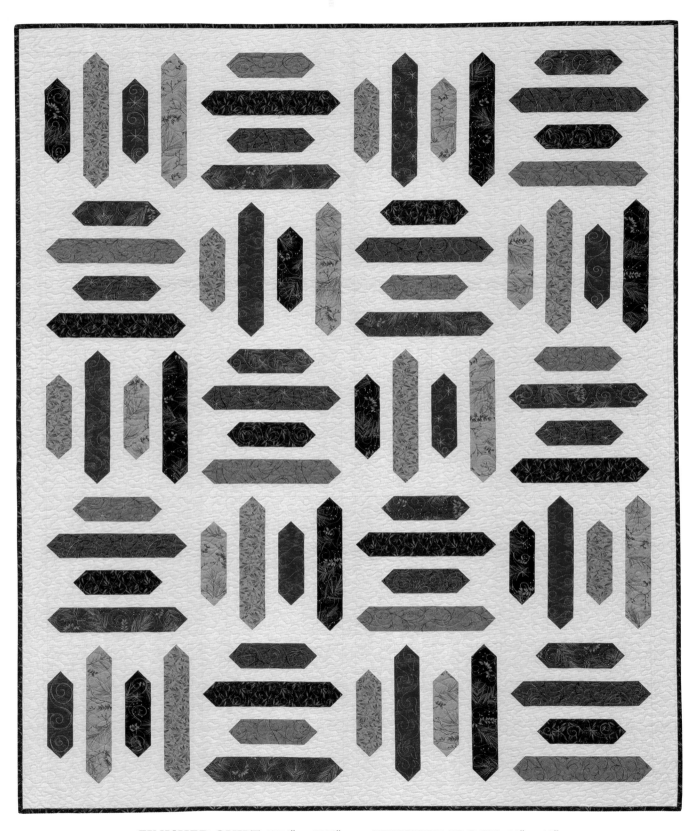

FINISHED QUILT: 51½" × 63½" ∼ **FINISHED BLOCK:** 11" × 11"
Pieced by Doug Leko; quilted by Sandy Pluff

Making the Blocks

Press all seam allowances as indicated by the arrows.

1 Draw a line from corner to corner on the wrong side of the cream 1½" squares. Place a marked square on the upper-left corner of a print 2½" × 11½" rectangle, right sides together. Stitch on the drawn line. Trim away the excess corner fabric, leaving a ¼" seam allowance. Place a marked square on the upper-right corner of the rectangle. Sew and trim as before. Make 40.

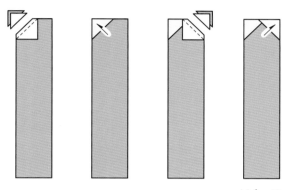

Make 40.

2 Repeat step 1, sewing marked squares to the remaining two corners of the print rectangle to complete an A unit. The unit should measure 2½" × 11½". Make 40 units.

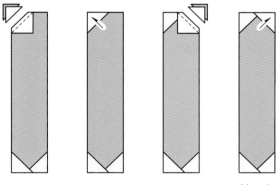

Unit A.
Make 40 units,
2½" × 11½".

3 Place a marked cream square from step 1 in the upper-left corner of a print 2½" × 7½" rectangle, right sides together. Stitch on the drawn line. Trim away the excess corner fabric, leaving a ¼" seam allowance. Place a marked square on the upper-right corner of the rectangle. Sew and trim as before. Make 40.

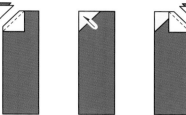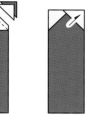

Make 40.

4 Repeat step 3, sewing marked squares to the remaining two corners of the print rectangle to complete a unit. The unit should measure 2½" × 7½". Make 40 units.

Make 40.

5 Sew a cream 2½" square to each end of a step 4 unit to make a B unit. The unit should measure 2½" × 11½". Make 40 units.

Unit B.
Make 40 units,
2½" × 11½".

6 Join an A unit, a B unit, and a cream 1½" × 11½" rectangle to make a C unit. The unit should measure 5½" × 11½". Make 40 units.

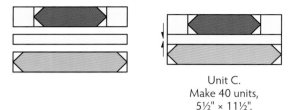

Unit C.
Make 40 units,
5½" × 11½".

7 Join two C units and one cream 1½" × 11½" rectangle to complete one block. The block should measure 11½" square, including seam allowances. Make 20 blocks.

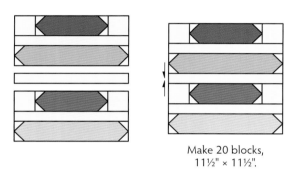

Make 20 blocks,
11½" × 11½".

Assembling the Quilt Top

1 Lay out the blocks in five rows of four blocks each, rotating them as shown in the quilt assembly diagram above right. Place a cream 1½" × 11½" rectangle between each of the blocks. Lay out the remaining cream 1½" × 11½" rectangles and cream 1½" squares in sashing rows, placing them between each of the block rows as shown.

2 Sew the pieces together into rows. Join the rows to complete the quilt-top center. The quilt top should measure 47½" × 59½", including the seam allowances.

3 Join the cream 2½"-wide strips end to end using diagonal seams. From the pieced strip, cut two 59½"-long strips and two 51½"-long strips. Sew the 59½"-long strips to opposite sides of the quilt. Sew the 51½"-long strips to the top and bottom of the quilt to complete the border.

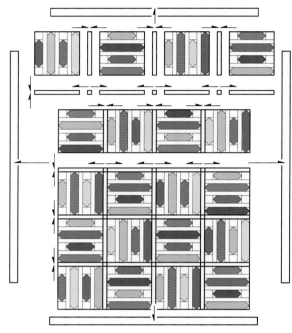

Quilt assembly

Finishing

For more details on any of the following steps, go to ShopMartingale.com/HowtoQuilt for free downloadable information.

1 Layer the quilt top with batting and backing. Baste the layers together.

2 Hand or machine quilt. The quilt shown is quilted with swirls and loops, plus stippling in the background. Trim the batting and backing so the edges are even with the quilt top.

3 Use the dark 2¼"-wide strips to make the binding, and then attach it to the quilt.

Alternate Colorway

Make this quilt extra fun by using scraps. Amp up the scrappiness by making the binding scrappy too. To make the scrappy binding, cut 12 strips, 2¼" × 21", from your fat quarters.

Pieced by Doug Leko; quilted by Sandy Pluff

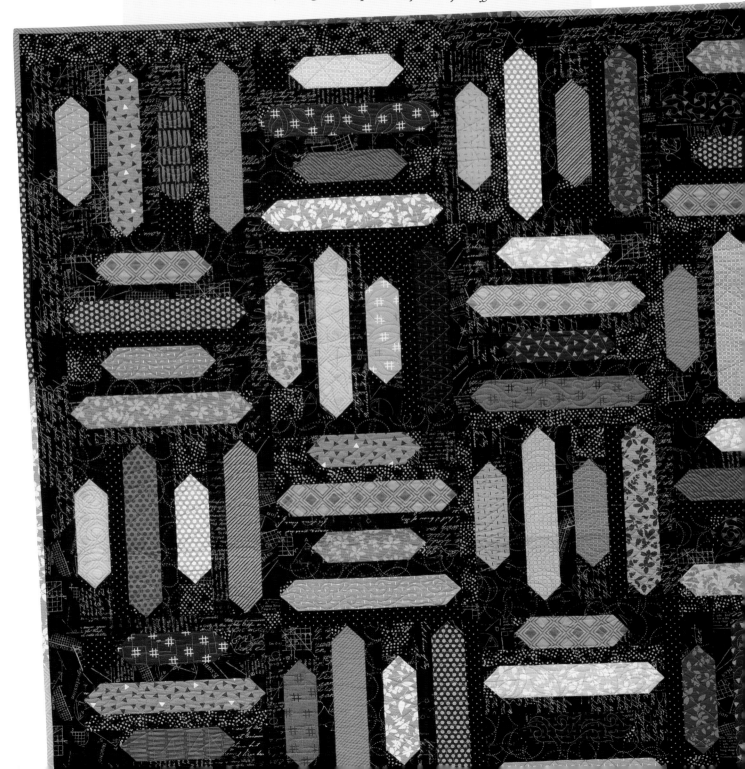

Honeycomb

Wouldn't this make a great "I Spy" quilt if you pieced it with lots of fun novelty prints? Think of all the possibilities.

Materials

Yardage is based on 42"-wide fabric. Fat quarters measure 18" × 21".

8 fat quarters of assorted red prints for blocks

8 fat quarters of assorted blue prints for blocks

3⅜ yards of cream print for blocks, sashing, and inner border

⅜ yard of navy print for middle border

1⅝ yards of red floral for outer border

⅝ yard of red solid for binding

7 yards of fabric for backing

83" × 99" piece of batting

Cutting

All measurements include ¼"-wide seam allowances.

From *each* red and blue fat quarter, cut:

1 strip, 6½" × 21"; crosscut into 1 square, 6½" × 6½" (16 total)

1 strip, 4½" × 21"; crosscut into 8 rectangles, 2½" × 4½" (128 total)

1 strip, 2½" × 21"; crosscut into 4 rectangles, 2½" × 4½" (64 total)

From the cream print, cut:

1 strip, 18½" × 42"; crosscut into:
- ⋄ 12 strips, 1½" × 18½"
- ⋄ 12 strips, 1½" × 14½"

4 strips, 6½" × 42"; crosscut into 64 rectangles, 2½" × 6½"

6 strips, 4½" × 42"; crosscut into 96 rectangles, 2½" × 4½"

10 strips, 2½" × 42"; crosscut into 160 squares, 2½" × 2½"

8 strips, 1½" × 42"; crosscut *1 of the strips* into 9 squares, 1½" × 1½"

From the navy print, cut:

8 strips, 1¼" × 42"

From the red floral, cut:

8 strips, 6½" × 42"

From the red solid, cut:

9 strips, 2¼" × 42"

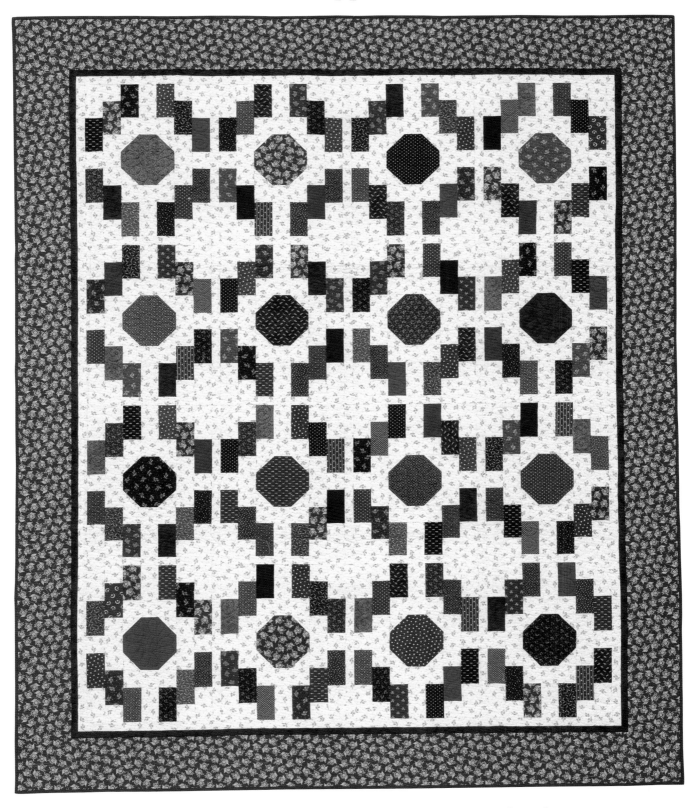

FINISHED QUILT: 75" × 91" ∿ **FINISHED BLOCK:** 14" × 18"
Pieced by Doug Leko; quilted by Sandy Pluff

Making the Blocks

Press all seam allowances as indicated by the arrows.

1 Draw a line from corner to corner on the wrong side of 64 cream 2½" squares. Place a marked square on each corner of a blue (or red) 6½" square, right sides together. Stitch on the drawn lines. Trim away the excess corner fabric, leaving a ¼" seam allowance. The unit should measure 6½" square. Make 16 center units.

Make 16 units,
6½" × 6½".

2 Join one blue, one cream, and one red 2½" × 4½" rectangle to make a 4½" × 6½" unit. Sew a cream 2½" × 6½" rectangle to the bottom of the unit to make a 6½" square. Make 32 units.

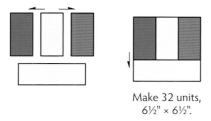

Make 32 units,
6½" × 6½".

3 Join two step 2 units to opposite ends of a center unit to make an A unit. The unit should measure 6½" × 18½". Make 16 units.

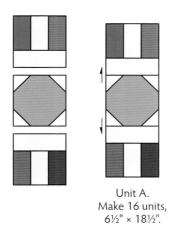

Unit A.
Make 16 units,
6½" × 18½".

4 Join a red (or blue) rectangle and a cream 2½" × 4½" rectangle end to end. The unit should measure 2½" × 8½". Make 64 units.

Make 64 units,
2½" × 8½".

5 Join a cream 2½" square and a blue (or red) rectangle. The unit should measure 2½" × 6½". Make 64 units.

Make 64 units,
2½" × 6½".

6 Lay out one red unit and one blue unit from step 5 and one cream 2½" × 6½" rectangle, making sure to place the blue unit at the top as shown. Lay out one red unit and one blue unit from step 4 and one cream 2½" square, making sure to place the red unit at the top. Sew the pieces together into vertical rows. Join the rows to make a B unit. The unit should measure 4½" × 18½". Make 32 units.

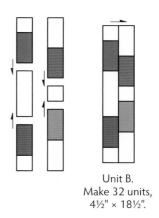

Unit B.
Make 32 units,
4½" × 18½".

7 Sew B units to opposite sides of an A unit, making sure to alternate the placement of the red and blue rectangles, to complete one block. The block should measure 14½" × 18½", including the seam allowances. Make 16 blocks.

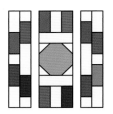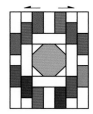

Make 16 blocks,
14½" × 18½".

Assembling the Quilt Top

1 Lay out the blocks in four rows of four blocks each, making sure to alternate the red and blue center units as shown in the quilt assembly diagram at right. Place a cream 1½" × 18½" strip between each of the blocks. Lay out the cream 1½" × 14½" strips and cream 1½" squares in sashing rows, placing them between each of the block rows as shown. Sew the pieces together into rows. Join the rows to complete the quilt-top center. The quilt should measure 59½" × 75½", including the seam allowances.

2 Join the cream 1½"-wide strips end to end using diagonal seams. From the pieced strip, cut two 75½"-long strips and two 61½"-long strips. Sew the 75½"-long strips to opposite sides of the quilt. Sew the 61½"-long strips to the top and bottom of the quilt to complete the inner border. The quilt top should measure 61½" × 77½", including the seam allowances.

3 Join the navy 1¼"-wide strips end to end using diagonal seams. From the pieced strip, cut two 77½"-long strips and two 63"-long strips. Sew the 77½"-long strips to opposite sides of the quilt. Sew the 63"-long strips to the top and bottom of the quilt to complete the middle border. The quilt top should measure 63" × 79", including the seam allowances.

4 Join the red floral 6½"-wide strips end to end using diagonal seams. From the pieced strip, cut two 79"-long and two 75"-long strips. Sew the 79"-long strips to opposite sides of the quilt. Sew the 75"-long strips to the top and bottom of the quilt to complete the outer border.

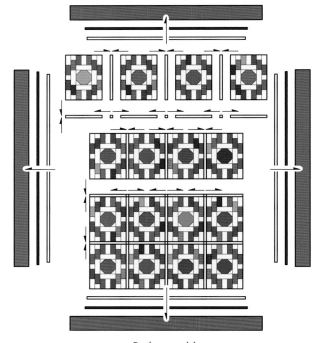

Quilt assembly

Finishing

For more details on any of the following steps, go to ShopMartingale.com/HowtoQuilt for free downloadable information.

1 Layer the quilt top with batting and backing. Baste the layers together.

2 Hand or machine quilt. The quilt shown is quilted with swirls, loops, and stippling in the blocks, and a feather motif in the border. Trim the batting and backing so the edges are even with the quilt top.

3 Use the red solid 2¼"-wide strips to make the binding, and then attach it to the quilt.

Alternate Colorway

Instead of fat quarters, head to your scrap bins and pull a collection of fabrics to make this quilt. For the blocks, you'll need 2½ yards of assorted prints or scraps, cut into a total of 16 squares, 6½" × 6½", and 192 rectangles, 2½" × 4½".

Pieced by Doug Leko; quilted by Sandy Pluff

Cathedral Ceiling

Don't be intimidated by the number of pieces in these blocks. Think of it as a block-of-the-month project and enjoy the process.

Materials

Yardage is based on 42"-wide fabric. Fat quarters measure 18" × 21".

11 fat quarters of assorted bright prints for blocks
6½ yards of black solid for blocks, sashing, border, and binding
5¾ yards of fabric for backing
73" × 94" piece of batting

Cutting

All measurements include ¼"-wide seam allowances.

From *each* bright fat quarter, cut:

2 strips, 3½" × 21"; crosscut into 6 squares, 3½" × 3½". Cut the squares into quarters diagonally to yield 24 B triangles (264 total).
3 strips, 2½" × 21"; crosscut into:
⋄ 19 squares, 2½" × 2½" (209 total)
⋄ 4 squares, 1¾" × 1¾" (44 total)

From the black solid, cut:

1 strip, 10⅞" × 42"; crosscut into 2 rectangles, 10⅞" × 20"
3 strips, 8" × 42"; crosscut into 11 squares, 8" × 8". Cut the squares into quarters diagonally to yield 44 C triangles.
9 strips, 7" × 42"; crosscut into 44 squares, 7" × 7"
3 strips, 4½" × 42"; crosscut into 22 squares, 4½" × 4½". Cut the squares in half diagonally to yield 44 A triangles.
3 strips, 3½" × 42"; crosscut into 33 squares, 3½" × 3½". Cut the squares into quarters diagonally to yield 132 B triangles.
15 strips, 2½" × 42"; crosscut into:
⋄ 198 squares, 2½" × 2½"
⋄ 44 rectangles, 1¾" × 2½"
9 strips, 1¾" × 42"; crosscut *4 of the strips* into 8 rectangles, 1¾" × 20"
16 strips, 2¼" × 42"

FINISHED QUILT: 65" × 85¾" ～ **FINISHED BLOCK:** 19½" × 19½"
Pieced by Elaine Leko and Janet Moser; quilted by Sandy Pluff

Making the Blocks

Use the squares from one print to make each block. Directions are for making one block. Repeat to make a total of 11 blocks. Press all seam allowances as indicated by the arrows.

1 Lay out four bright 1¾" squares, four black 1¾" × 2½" rectangles, and one bright 2½" square in three rows as shown. Sew the pieces together into rows. Join the rows to make a unit that measures 5" square.

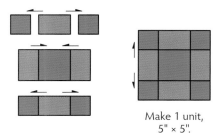

Make 1 unit,
5" × 5".

2 Center and sew a black A triangle on each side of the step 1 unit to make a center unit. Square up the unit to measure 7" square, including seam allowances.

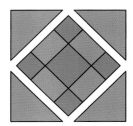 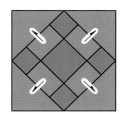

Make 1 unit,
7" × 7".

3 Referring to "Half-Square-Triangle Units" on page 79, use 18 black and 18 bright 2½" squares to make a total of 36 units. Press the seam allowances on 24 units toward the bright triangles. Press the seam allowances on the remaining 12 units toward the black triangles. Trim all units to measure 2" square, including seam allowances.

Make 24 units,
2" × 2".

Make 12 units,
2" × 2".

4 Using the half-square-triangle units with the seam allowances pressed toward the black triangles, lay out three units and three black B triangles in three rows as shown. Join the pieces in the top and middle rows. Sew the rows together. Sew a B triangle to the bottom of the unit to make a triangular unit. Make four units.

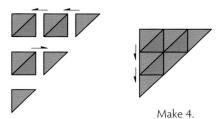

Make 4.

5 Using the half-square-triangle units with the seam allowances pressed toward the bright triangles, lay out three units and three bright B triangles in three rows as shown. Repeat step 4 to make a triangular unit. Make eight units.

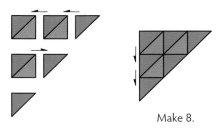

Make 8.

6 Join one step 4 unit, two step 5 units, and one black C triangle to make a side unit. Square up the unit to measure 7" square, including seam allowances. Make four units.

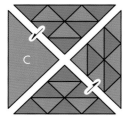 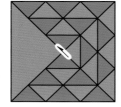

Make 4 units,
7" × 7".

7 Lay out four black 7" squares, four side units, and one center unit in three rows. Sew the pieces together into rows. Join the rows to complete one block. The block should measure 20" square, including the seam allowances. Make a total of 11 blocks.

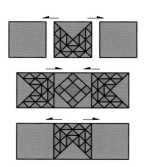 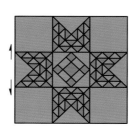

Make 11 blocks,
20" × 20".

Assembling the Quilt Top

1 Lay out the blocks, black 1¾" × 20" rectangles, and black 10⅞" × 20" rectangles in three vertical rows as shown in the quilt assembly diagram above right. Join the pieces in each row. Make three rows measuring 20" × 82¼", including the seam allowances.

2 Join the remaining five black 1¾"-wide strips end to end using diagonal seams. From the pieced strip, cut two 82¼"-long sashing strips. Join the sashing strips and block rows to complete the quilt-top center. The quilt top should measure 61½" × 82¼", including the seam allowances.

3 Join eight black 2¼"-wide strips end to end using diagonal seams. From the pieced strip, cut two 82¼"-long and two 65"-long strips. Sew the 82¼"-long strips to opposite sides of the quilt top. Sew the 65"-long strips to the top and bottom of the quilt to complete the border.

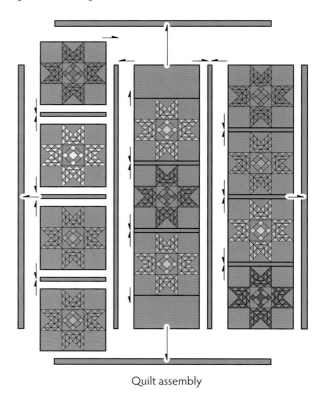

Quilt assembly

Finishing

For more details on any of the following steps, go to ShopMartingale.com/HowtoQuilt for free downloadable information.

1 Layer the quilt top with batting and backing. Baste the layers together.

2 Hand or machine quilt. The quilt shown is quilted with an overall design of swirls and feathered plumes. Trim the batting and backing so the edges are even with the quilt top.

3 Use the remaining black 2¼"-wide strips to make the binding, and then attach it to the quilt.

Alternate Colorway

I wanted to use 1930s reproduction prints for this quilt, but rather than use a white background, I selected a solid buttercream. Isn't it amazing what color choice and placement do for a quilt design?

Pieced by Elaine Leko and Janet Moser; quilted by Sandy Pluff

Due North

If you struggle with piecing flying geese, you'll love this quilt. The geese units are pieced slightly oversized so that they can be trimmed to the perfect size. No more clipping the wings or cutting off the points!

Materials

Yardage is based on 42"-wide fabric. Fat quarters measure 18" × 21".

3½ yards of light print for background

14 fat quarters of assorted prints for flying-geese units

½ yard of gray print for binding

4⅛ yards of fabric for backing

67" × 79" piece of batting

Cutting

All measurements include ¼"-wide seam allowances.

From the light print, cut:

2 strips, 8½" × 42"; crosscut into 8 squares, 8½" × 8½"

4 strips, 6½" × 42"; crosscut into 24 squares, 6½" × 6½"

7 strips, 5" × 42"; crosscut into 56 squares, 5" × 5"

1 strip, 4½" × 42"; crosscut into 8 squares, 4½" × 4½"

10 strips, 3" × 42"; crosscut into 128 squares, 3" × 3"

From *each* print fat quarter, cut:

1 rectangle, 6½" × 12½" (14 total; 2 will be extra)

1 square, 9½" × 9½" (14 total)

3 squares, 5½" × 5½" (42 total; 10 will be extra)

From the gray print, cut:

7 strips, 2¼" × 42"

FINISHED QUILT: 60½" × 72½"
Pieced by Doug Leko; quilted by Sandy Pluff

Making the Flying-Geese Units

Press all seam allowances as indicated by the arrows.

1 Draw a line from corner to corner on the wrong side of the light 6½" squares. Place a marked square on one end of a print 6½" × 12½" rectangle, right sides together. Stitch on the drawn line. Trim away the excess corner fabric, leaving a ¼" seam allowance. Place a marked light square on the other end of the print rectangle, right sides together. Stitch and trim as before. The unit should measure 6½" × 12½". Make 12 of unit A.

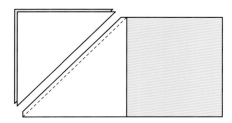

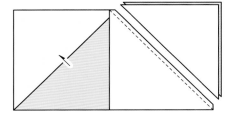

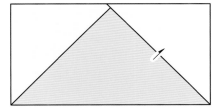

Unit A.
Make 12 units,
6½" × 12½".

2 Referring to "Flying-Geese Units" on page 78, use the light 5" squares and print 9½" squares to make 56 of unit B. Trim the units to measure 4½" × 8½".

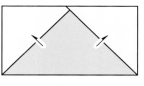

Unit B.
Make 56 units,
4½" × 8½".

3 In the same manner as for step 2, use the light 3" squares and print 5½" squares to make 128 of unit C. Trim the units to measure 2½" × 4½".

Unit C.
Make 128 units,
2½" × 4½".

Assembling the Quilt Top

1 Join 14 of unit B and two light 8½" squares to make a vertical row as shown in the quilt assembly diagram on page 34. The row should measure 8½" × 72½", including the seam allowances. Make four of these rows for rows 1, 3, 7, and 9, noting that the placement of the light squares is different in each row.

2 Join 32 of unit C and two light 4½" squares to make a vertical row as shown in the quilt assembly diagram. The row should measure 4½" × 72½", including seam allowances. Make four of these rows for rows 2, 4, 6, and 8, noting that the placement of the light squares is different in each row.

3 Join 12 of unit A to make vertical row 5 that measures 12½" × 72½", including seam allowances.

4 Sew the rows together to complete the quilt top.

5 Stitch around the perimeter of the quilt top, ⅛" from the edges, to lock the seams in place.

Finishing

For more details on any of the following steps, go to ShopMartingale.com/HowtoQuilt for free downloadable information.

1 Layer the quilt top with batting and backing. Baste the layers together.

2 Hand or machine quilt. The quilt shown is quilted with double paisleys and elongated loops. Trim the batting and backing so the edges are even with the quilt top.

3 Use the gray 2¼"-wide strips to make the binding, and then attach it to the quilt.

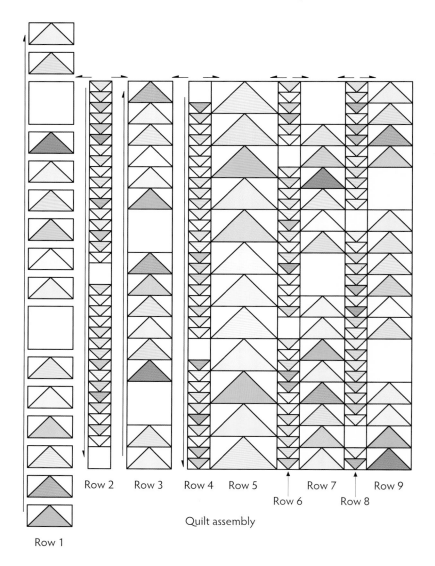

Row 1 Row 2 Row 3 Row 4 Row 5 Row 6 Row 7 Row 8 Row 9

Quilt assembly

Alternate Colorway

In this version, it's not just the geese that are scrappy—the background is too. You'll need 14 fat quarters of assorted light prints (rather than 3½ yards of one fabric) to make a scrappy background.

Pieced by Doug Leko; quilted by Sandy Pluff

Country Roads

Here's my version of one of the oldest quilt blocks, the Log Cabin. It's arranged in an asymmetrical layout, one of my favorite settings. Because each block is the same, you can twist and turn them to design your own layout if you want to be different!

Materials

Yardage is based on 42"-wide fabric. Fat quarters measure 18" × 21".

½ yard *each* of 8 assorted light prints for blocks
27 fat quarters of assorted prints for blocks
⅝ yard of purple print for binding
5½ yards of fabric for backing
73" × 89" piece of batting

Cutting

All measurements include ¼"-wide seam allowances.

From *each* light print, cut:

1 strip, 7½" × 42"; crosscut into:
  ◊ 10 rectangles, 1" × 7½" (80 total)
  ◊ 10 rectangles, 1" × 7" (80 total)
  ◊ 10 rectangles, 1" × 6" (80 total)
  ◊ 10 rectangles, 1" × 5½" (80 total)
1 strip, 4½" × 42"; crosscut into:
  ◊ 10 rectangles, 1" × 4½" (80 total)
  ◊ 10 rectangles, 1" × 4" (80 total)
  ◊ 10 rectangles, 1" × 3" (80 total)
  ◊ 10 rectangles, 1" × 2½" (80 total)
1 strip, 2½" × 42"; crosscut into 10 squares,
  2½" × 2½" (80 total)

From *each* print fat quarter, cut:

1 strip, 8½" × 21"; crosscut into:
  ◊ 3 rectangles, 1½" × 8½" (81 total; 1 will be extra)
  ◊ 3 rectangles, 1½" × 7½" (81 total; 1 will be extra)
  ◊ 3 rectangles, 1½" × 7" (81 total; 1 will be extra)
  ◊ 3 rectangles, 1½" × 6" (81 total; 1 will be extra)
1 strip, 5½" × 21"; crosscut into:
  ◊ 3 rectangles, 1½" × 5½" (81 total; 1 will be extra)
  ◊ 3 rectangles, 1½" × 4½" (81 total; 1 will be extra)
  ◊ 3 rectangles, 1½" × 4" (81 total; 1 will be extra)
  ◊ 3 rectangles, 1½" × 3" (81 total; 1 will be extra)

From the purple print, cut:

8 strips, 2¼" × 42"

Making the Blocks

Press all seam allowances as indicated by the arrows.

1. Join a light 1" × 2½" rectangle and a light square. Sew a light 1" × 3" rectangle to the top of the unit. The unit should measure 3" square. Make 80.

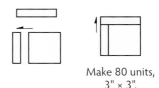

Make 80 units,
3" × 3".

FINISHED QUILT: 64½" × 80½" ～ **FINISHED BLOCK:** 8" × 8"
Pieced by Doug Leko and Janet Moser; quilted by Sandy Pluff

2 Sew a print 1½" × 3" rectangle to the right side of a step 1 unit. Sew a print 1½" × 4" rectangle to the bottom of the unit. The unit should measure 4" square. Make 80.

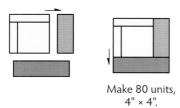

Make 80 units,
4" × 4".

3 Sew a light 1" × 4" rectangle to the left side of a step 2 unit. Sew a light 1" × 4½" rectangle to the top of the unit to make a 4½" square. Make 80.

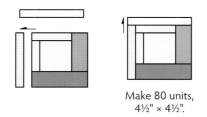

Make 80 units,
4½" × 4½".

4 Join a print 1½" × 4½" rectangle and a print 1½" × 5½" rectangle to a step 3 unit to make a 5½" square. Make 80.

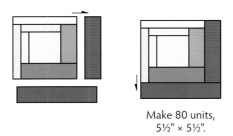

Make 80 units,
5½" × 5½".

5 Join a light 1" × 5½" rectangle and a light 1" × 6" rectangle to a step 4 unit to make a 6" square. Make 80.

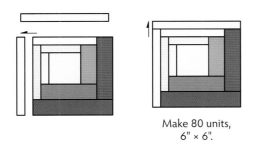

Make 80 units,
6" × 6".

6 Join a print 1½" × 6" rectangle and a print 1½" × 7" rectangle to a step 5 unit to make a 7" square. Make 80.

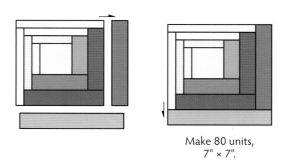

Make 80 units,
7" × 7".

7 Join a light 1" × 7" rectangle and a light 1" × 7½" rectangle to a step 6 unit to make a 7½" square. Make 80.

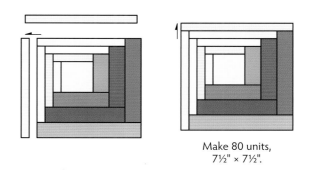

Make 80 units,
7½" × 7½".

8 Join a print 1½" × 7½" rectangle and a print 1½" × 8½" rectangle to a step 7 unit to complete one block. The block should measure 8½" square. Make 80 blocks.

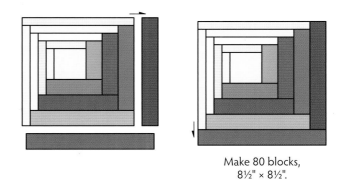

Make 80 blocks,
8½" × 8½".

Assembling the Quilt Top

1 Lay out the blocks in 10 rows of eight blocks each, rotating every other block in each row as shown in the quilt assembly diagram below. Sew the blocks together into rows.

2 Join the rows to complete the quilt-top center. Stitch around the perimeter of the quilt top, ⅛" from the outer edges, to lock the seams in place.

Finishing

For more details on any of the following steps, go to ShopMartingale.com/HowtoQuilt for free downloadable information.

1 Layer the quilt top with batting and backing. Baste the layers together.

2 Hand or machine quilt. The quilt shown is quilted with an overall feather design, plus stippling in the background. Trim the batting and backing so the edges are even with the quilt top.

3 Use the purple 2¼"-wide strips to make the binding, and then attach it to the quilt.

Quilt assembly

Alternate Colorway

To make an even scrappier version, I used more than 80 different prints. To accomplish the same look, use your scrap bins to collect as many fabrics as you want. Find the total number of pieces (listed in parentheses) for each size strip on page 37.

Pieced by Doug Leko and Janet Moser; quilted by Sandy Pluff

Short Circuit

Is your stash overflowing with odds and ends?
Put them all together and be amazed at how
well they work together in this quilt.

Materials

*Yardage is based on 42"-wide fabric. Fat quarters
measure 18" × 21".*

4 yards *total* of assorted cream prints for blocks
  and outer border
16 fat quarters of assorted prints for blocks, inner
  border, and binding
4⅛ yards of fabric for backing
67" × 79" piece of batting

Cutting

All measurements include ¼"-wide seam allowances.

From the cream prints, cut a *total* of:
12 strips, 5½" × 24"
14 rectangles, 5" × 6½"
14 rectangles, 2" × 3½"
132 squares, 3½" × 3½"
146 squares, 2" × 2"

From *each of 15* print fat quarters, cut:
1 strip, 3½" × 21"; crosscut into 9 rectangles, 2" × 3½"
  (135 total; 3 will be extra)
2 strips, 2" × 21"; crosscut into 19 squares, 2" × 2"
  (285 total; 7 will be extra)

**From the remaining assorted prints, cut a
total of:**
30 strips, 1½" × 9"
37 strips, 2¼" × 8½"

FINISHED QUILT: 60½" × 72½" ∽ **FINISHED BLOCK:** 6" × 6"
Pieced by Doug Leko; quilted by Sandy Pluff

Making Block A

Press all seam allowances as indicated by the arrows.

1 Join a cream 2" × 3½" rectangle, a print 2" square, and a cream 2" square to make a unit measuring 2" × 6½". Make 14 units.

Make 14 units,
2" × 6½".

2 Sew the unit from step 1 to one long side of a cream 5" × 6½" rectangle to complete one of block A. The block should measure 6½" square, including seam allowances. Make 14 blocks.

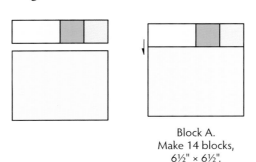

Block A.
Make 14 blocks,
6½" × 6½".

Making Block B

1 Draw a line from corner to corner on the wrong side of 132 print 2" squares. Place a marked square on one corner of a cream 3½" square, right sides together. Stitch on the drawn line. Trim away the excess corner fabric, leaving a ¼" seam allowance. The unit should measure 3½" square. Make 132 units.

Make 132 units,
3½" × 3½".

2 Join one print 2" square and one cream 2" square to make a unit measuring 2" × 3½". Make 132 units.

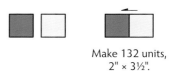

Make 132 units,
2" × 3½".

3 Sew a step 2 unit and a print 2" × 3½" rectangle together to make a unit that measures 3½" square. Make 132 units.

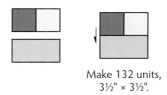

Make 132 units,
3½" × 3½".

4 Lay out two units from step 1 and two units from step 3 in two rows, rotating them as shown. Sew the units together into rows. Join the rows to complete one of block B. See "Spin the Seam Allowances" on page 79 for pressing information. The block should measure 6½" square, including the seam allowances. Make 66 blocks.

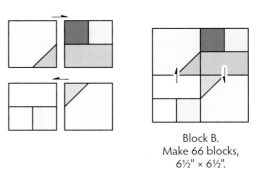

Block B.
Make 66 blocks,
6½" × 6½".

Assembling the Quilt Top

1 Lay out the A and B blocks in 10 rows of eight blocks each, rotating the blocks as shown in the quilt assembly diagram below. Sew the blocks together into rows. Join the rows to complete the quilt-top center. The quilt top should measure 48½" × 60½".

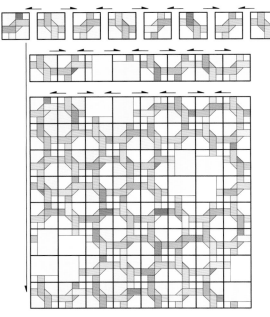

Quilt assembly

2 Join the print 1½" × 9" strips end to end using diagonal seams. From the pieced strip, cut two 60½"-long strips and two 50½"-long strips. Sew the 60½"-long strips to opposite sides of the quilt top. Sew the 50½"-long strips to the top and bottom of the quilt to complete the inner border. The quilt should measure 50½" × 62½", including the seam allowances.

3 Using diagonal seams, join three light 5½"-wide strips end to end to make a border strip. Make four strips. From the pieced strips, cut

two 62½"-long strips and two 60½"-long strips. Sew the 62½"-long strips to opposite sides of the quilt top. Sew the 60½"-long strips to the top and bottom of the quilt to complete the outer border.

Adding borders

Finishing

For more details on any of the following steps, go to ShopMartingale.com/HowtoQuilt for free downloadable information.

1 Layer the quilt top with batting and backing. Baste the layers together.

2 Hand or machine quilt. The quilt shown is quilted with circles, curved diamonds, switchbacks, and stippling in the background; with a meandering design in the colorful pieces; and with loops in the inner border. Trim the batting and backing so the edges are even with the quilt top.

3 Use the assorted print 2¼" × 8½" strips to make the binding, and then attach it to the quilt.

Alternate Colorway

For a spooky version, use Halloween novelty prints and a single background fabric rather than an assortment of prints. You'll need 2⅜ yards of light fabric for the background, ⅜ yard for the inner border, 1¼ yards for the outer border, and ½ yard for the binding.

From the inner-border fabric, cut:
6 strips, 1½" × 42"

From the outer-border fabric, cut:
7 strips, 5½" × 42"

From the binding fabric, cut:
7 strips, 2¼" × 42"

Pieced by Janet Moser; quilted by Sandy Pluff

French Twist

One word to describe this quilt is *fun!* A flexible pattern, it looks just as good made of many colors as it does made from only two, as shown on page 53.

Materials

Yardage is based on 42"-wide fabric. Fat quarters measure 18" × 21".

3⅝ yards of light print for blocks and sashing
20 fat quarters of assorted prints for blocks and sashing squares
⅝ yard of dark print for binding
5¾ yards of fabric for backing
77" × 93" piece of batting

Cutting

All measurements include ¼"-wide seam allowances.

From the light print, cut:
3 strips, 15" × 42"; crosscut into 48 rectangles, 2½" × 15"
8 strips, 4¾" × 42"; crosscut into 60 squares, 4¾" × 4¾". Cut the squares into quarters diagonally to yield 240 B triangles.
5 strips, 4½" × 42"; crosscut into 40 squares, 4½" × 4½". Cut the squares in half diagonally to yield 80 C triangles.
4 strips, 3¼" × 42"; crosscut into:
  ◇ 40 squares, 3¼" × 3¼"; cut the squares in half diagonally to yield 80 A triangles
  ◇ 1 rectangle, 2½" × 15"

From *each* print fat quarter, cut:
1 strip, 6½" × 21"; crosscut into 8 rectangles, 2½" × 6½" (160 total)
1 strip, 4½" × 21"; crosscut into:
  ◇ 4 rectangles, 2½" × 4½" (80 total)
  ◇ 1 square, 3⅜" × 3⅜" (20 total)
1 strip, 2½" × 21"; crosscut into 6 squares, 2½" × 2½" (120 total; 10 will be extra)

From the dark print, cut:
8 strips, 2¼" × 42"

Making the Blocks

Press all seam allowances as indicated by the arrows.

1 Center and sew a light A triangle on each side of a print 3⅜" square to make a center unit. Trim the unit to measure 4½" square, including seam allowances. Make 20.

 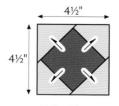

Make 20 units.

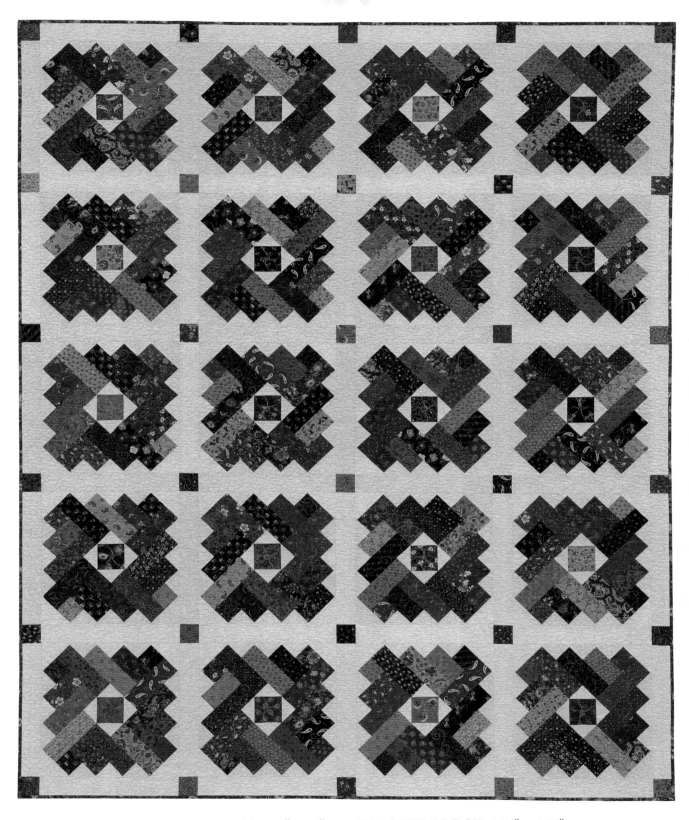

FINISHED QUILT: 68½" × 85" ∾ **FINISHED BLOCK:** 14½" × 14½"
Pieced by Elaine Leko; quilted by Sandy Pluff

2 Sew a light B triangle to the right end of a print 2½" × 6½" rectangle. Make 80 units.

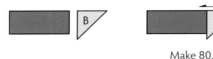

Make 80.

3 Sew a light B triangle to the right end of a print 2½" × 4½" rectangle. Make 80 units.

Make 80.

4 Sew a light B triangle to a print 2½" square as shown. Make 80 units.

Make 80.

5 Join one unit each from steps 2, 3, and 4 as shown. Sew a print 2½" × 6½" rectangle onto the left side of the three-piece unit to make a strip unit. Make 80 units.

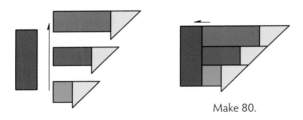

Make 80.

6 Place a center unit on the upper-right corner of a strip unit from step 5, right sides together. Start stitching at the top edge and stop about 1" from the end of the center unit. Make 20.

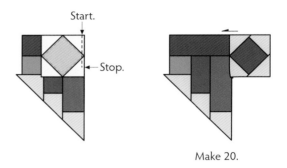

Make 20.

7 Sew a strip unit to the top of the unit from step 6, sewing all the way across the units. Then sew a strip unit to the right side. Make 20.

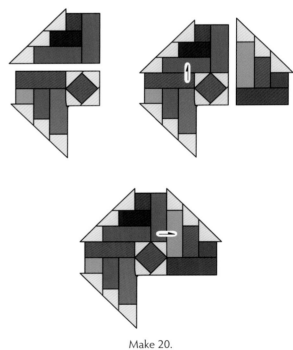

Make 20.

Trim the Tips

You can trim the dog-ears as you go or let them flap in the wind and ignore them. It's your choice.

8 Sew a strip unit to the bottom. Then finish sewing the seam of the open section of the center-unit seam closed to complete the unit. Make 20.

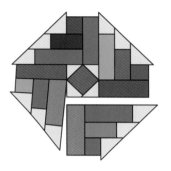 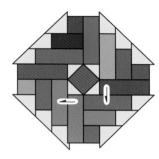

Make 20.

9 Sew a light C triangle to each corner of a step 8 unit to complete the block, making sure each C triangle is centered. Trim and square up the block to measure 15" square, leaving ⅜" beyond the points all around the block for seam allowances. Make 20 blocks.

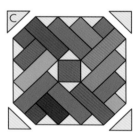 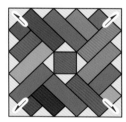

Make 20 blocks,
15" × 15".

Assembling the Quilt Top

1 Lay out the blocks in five rows of four blocks each. Place a light 2½" × 15" rectangle between each of the blocks. Lay out the light 2½" × 15" rectangles and print 2½" squares in sashing rows, placing them between each of the block rows as shown in the quilt assembly diagram above right. Sew the pieces together into rows.

2 Join the rows to complete the quilt-top center. Stitch around the perimeter of the quilt top, ⅛" from the outer edges, to lock the seams in place.

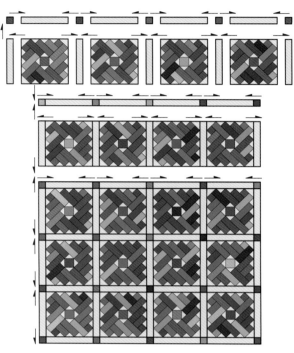

Quilt assembly

Finishing

For more details on any of the following steps, go to ShopMartingale.com/HowtoQuilt for free downloadable information.

1 Layer the quilt top with batting and backing. Baste the layers together.

2 Hand or machine quilt. The quilt shown is quilted with an overall design of swirls, leaves, and petals. Trim the batting and backing so the edges are even with the quilt top.

3 Use the dark 2¼"-wide strips to make the binding, and then attach it to the quilt.

Alternate Colorway

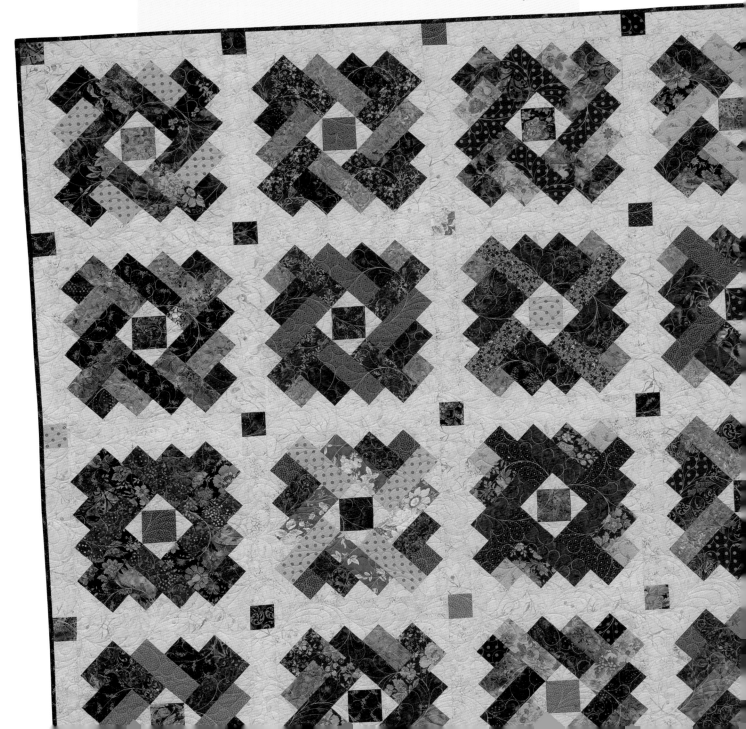

This version of French Twist is a "Doug-planned scrappy," meaning I made things in fours. That is, while each block is different from the others, each quadrant of a block uses the same fabrics in the same positions. If you struggle with making a truly scrappy quilt, try this method and see how you like it.

Pieced by Doug Leko and Janet Moser; quilted by Nicole Christoffersen

Classic Mosaic

It was so much fun to see the block evolve while piecing this quilt. I became obsessed with the color placement and watching each new combination come to life. Strip piecing saves you from cutting lots of small pieces, so grab your scrap bin and get started!

Materials

Yardage is based on 42"-wide fabric. Fat quarters measure 18" × 21".

3¼ yards of cream print for blocks and sashing
22 fat quarters of assorted prints for blocks and setting triangles
⅝ yard of brown print for binding
5½ yards of fabric for backing
71" × 87" piece of batting

Cutting

All measurements include ¼"-wide seam allowances.

From the cream print, cut:
4 strips, 10½" × 42"; crosscut into 80 strips, 1½" × 10½"
6 strips, 3½" × 42"; crosscut into 22 strips, 3½" × 10"
28 strips, 1½" × 42"; crosscut into:
 ◇ 44 strips, 1½" × 18"
 ◇ 22 strips, 1½" × 10"

From *each of 14* print fat quarters, cut:
1 A triangle (14 total)*

From *each of 4* print fat quarters, cut:
1 B triangle (4 total)*

From *each of 5* print fat quarters, cut:
7 squares, 1½" × 1½" (35 total; 4 will be extra)
1 square, 3" × 3"; cut into quarters diagonally to yield 4 C triangles (20 total; 2 will be extra)

From *each* print fat quarter, cut:
2 strips, 3½" × 18" (44 total)
2 strips, 1½" × 18" (44 total)
1 strip, 1½" × 10" (22 total)

From the brown print, cut:
8 strips, 2¼" × 42"

Refer to "Cutting the Triangles" on page 58.

FINISHED QUILT: 62¾" × 78⅜" ∼ **FINISHED BLOCK:** 10" × 10"
Pieced by Doug Leko and Janet Moser; quilted by Nicole Christoffersen

Making the Blocks

Press all seam allowances as indicated by the arrows.

1 Join a print 1½" × 18" strip, a cream 1½" × 18" strip, and a matching print 3½" × 18" strip along their long edges to make a strip set. Make 44 strip sets. Crosscut each strip set into three 1½" × 5½" segments and three 3½" × 5½" segments.

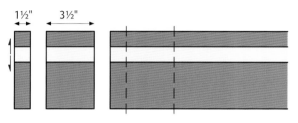

Make 44 strip sets.
Cut 3 segments, 1½" × 5½", and
3 segments, 3½" × 5½".

2 Join a cream 1½" × 10" strip, a print 1½" × 10" strip, and a cream 3½" × 10" strip along their long edges to make a strip set. Make 22 strip sets. Crosscut each strip set into six 1½" × 5½" segments.

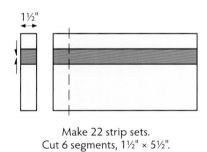

Make 22 strip sets.
Cut 6 segments, 1½" × 5½".

3 Lay out a 1½"-wide segment and a 3½"-wide segment from step 1 and a segment from step 2 as shown; all the prints should match. Join the segments to make a quadrant. The quadrant should measure 5½" square. Make 128 quadrants. (You'll have four step 1 segments in each width and four step 2 segments left over for another project.)

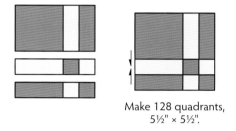

Make 128 quadrants,
5½" × 5½".

4 Lay out four quadrants in two rows, rotating them as shown. Join the quadrants into rows. Join the rows to complete one block. See "Spin the Seam Allowances" on page 79 for help on pressing for nice, flat blocks. The block should measure 10½" square, including seam allowances. Make 32 blocks.

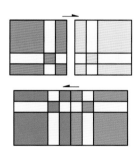
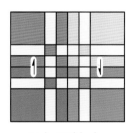

Make 32 blocks,
10½" × 10½".

Cutting the Triangles

I wanted the A and B setting triangles to be as scrappy as the rest of the quilt, so I used a template instead of cutting four identical quarter-square triangles (or two identical half-square triangles) from a large square.

To make a quarter-square-triangle template, draw a 16" square on a large piece of paper. Cut out the square, and then cut the square into quarters diagonally to make four quarter-square triangles. Use one of the paper templates to cut an A triangle from each of 14 different fat quarters, making sure to place the long side of the triangle on the straight of grain.

To make a half-square-triangle template, draw a 9" square on a large piece of paper. Cut out the square, and then cut the square in half diagonally to make two half-square triangles. Use one of the paper templates to cut a B triangle from each of four different fat quarters, making sure to place the short side of the triangle on the straight of grain.

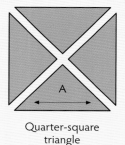

Quarter-square triangle

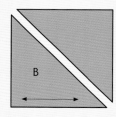

Half-square triangle

Assembling the Quilt Top

1 Lay out the blocks, cream 1½" × 10½" strips, print 1½" squares, and the A, B, and C triangles in diagonal rows as shown in the quilt assembly diagram above right. Sew the pieces together into rows.

2 Join the rows to complete the quilt top, adding the B triangles last. The A, B, and C triangles are cut slightly oversized for easier cutting and piecing. Trim and square up the quilt top, making sure to leave ¼" beyond the points of the sashing for seam allowances.

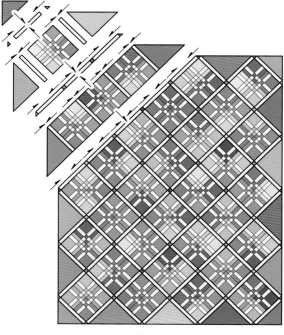

Quilt assembly

3 Stitch around the perimeter of the quilt top, ⅛" from the outer edges, to lock the seams in place.

Finishing

For more details on any of the following steps, go to ShopMartingale.com/HowtoQuilt for free downloadable information.

1 Layer the quilt top with batting and backing. Baste the layers together.

2 Hand or machine quilt. The quilt shown is quilted with a large overall feather design. Trim the batting and backing so the edges are even with the quilt top.

3 Use the brown 2¼"-wide strips to make the binding, and then attach it to the quilt.

Alternate Colorway

I love how different this quilt looks from the other colorway. I went to my candy-colored scraps and started cutting, finding that the more fabrics I used, the better the quilt looked.

Pieced by Doug Leko and Janet Moser; quilted by Nicole Christoffersen

Easy Street

We all appreciate quick quilts and look for them when we want to finish something fast. Give this pattern a try—it couldn't be easier.

Materials

Yardage is based on 42"-wide fabric. Fat quarters measure 18" × 21".

30 fat quarters of assorted prints for blocks
⅝ yard of red print for binding
4½ yards of fabric for backing
69" × 79" piece of batting

Cutting

All measurements include ¼"-wide seam allowances.

From *each* print fat quarter, cut:
1 strip, 6½" × 21"; crosscut into:
  ◇ 1 square, 6½" × 6½" (30 total)
  ◇ 3 rectangles, 3½" × 6½" (90 total)
2 strips, 3½" × 21"; crosscut into:
  ◇ 1 rectangle, 3½" × 6½" (30 total)
  ◇ 4 squares, 3½" × 3½" (120 total)

From the red print, cut:
7 strips, 2¼" × 42"

Making the Blocks

Press all seam allowances as indicated by the arrows.

1. Sew two print 3½" squares together to make a two-square unit. Sew a rectangle to the top of the unit. The completed unit should measure 6½" square. Make 30 units.

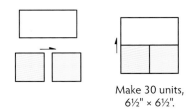

Make 30 units,
6½" × 6½".

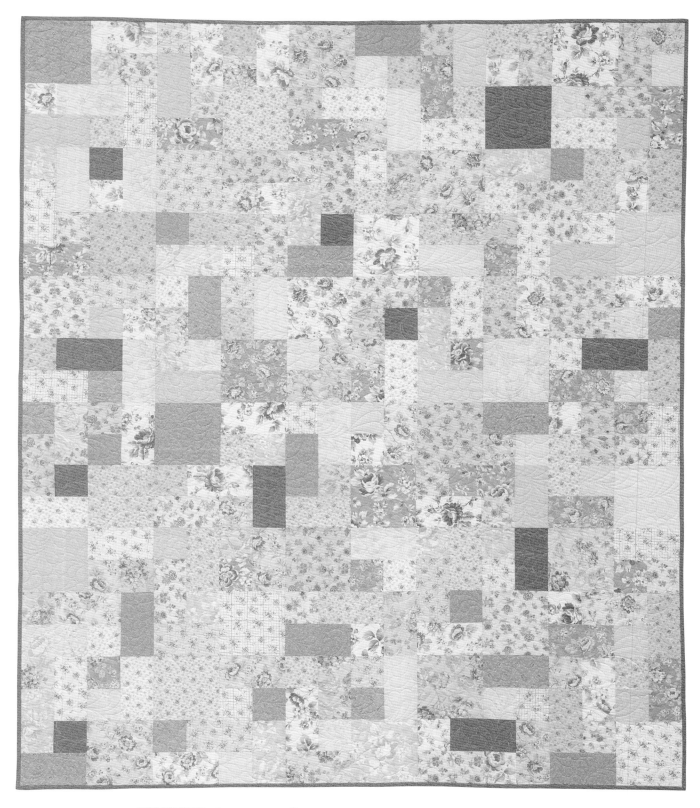

FINISHED QUILT: 60½" × 72½" ◠ **FINISHED BLOCK:** 12" × 12"
Pieced by Janet Moser; quilted by Nicole Christoffersen

2 Join a print 6½" square to the left side of a unit from step 1. The unit should measure 6½" × 12½". Make 15 units. Set aside the remaining step 1 units for step 6.

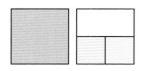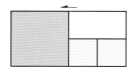

Make 15 units,
6½" × 12½".

3 Join a print 3½" square and a rectangle to make a unit measuring 3½" × 9½". Make 60 units.

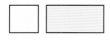

Make 60 units,
3½" × 9½".

4 Join two step 3 units along their long edges, making sure to position the units as shown. Add a rectangle to the right side of the unit. The completed unit should measure 6½" × 12½". Make 15 units.

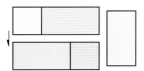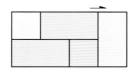

Make 15 units,
6½" × 12½".

5 Sew together units from step 2 and step 4 along their long edges to complete one of block A. The block should measure 12½" square, including the seam allowances. Make 15 blocks.

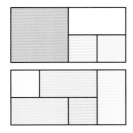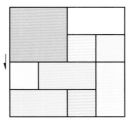

Block A.
Make 15 blocks,
12½" × 12½".

6 Join a print 6½" square to the right side of a step 1 unit. The unit should measure 6½" × 12½". Make 15 units.

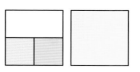

Make 15 units,
6½" × 12½".

7 Join two units from step 3 along their long edges, making sure to position the units as shown. Add a rectangle to the right side of the unit. The completed unit should measure 6½" × 12½". Make 15 units.

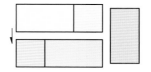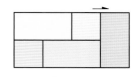

Make 15 units,
6½" × 12½".

8 Join units from steps 6 and 7 along their long edges to complete one of block B. The block should measure 12½" square, including the seam allowances. Make 15 blocks.

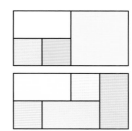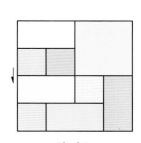

Block B.
Make 15 blocks,
12½" × 12½".

Assembling the Quilt Top

1 Lay out the A and B blocks in six rows of five blocks each, rotating the B blocks as shown in the quilt assembly diagram below. Sew the blocks together into rows.

2 Join the rows to complete the quilt top. Stitch around the perimeter of the quilt top, ⅛" from the outer edges, to lock the seams in place.

Finishing

For more details on any of the following steps, go to ShopMartingale.com/HowtoQuilt for free downloadable information.

1 Layer the quilt top with batting and backing. Baste the layers together.

2 Hand or machine quilt. The quilt shown is quilted with an overall feather design. Trim the batting and backing so the edges are even with the quilt top.

3 Use the red 2¼"-wide strips to make the binding, and then attach it to the quilt.

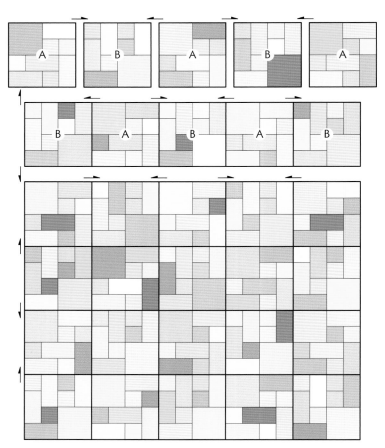

Quilt assembly

Alternate Colorway

For this version, I used my scraps of blue and yellow. There is nothing more relaxing than a blue-and-yellow quilt.

Pieced by Janet Moser; quilted by Nicole Christoffersen

Nine by Nine

Nine patches, need I say more? Pleasing to the eye and easy to stitch, they're even more fun in a mix of sizes. Here I used three different sizes. Can you spot the different versions?

Materials

Yardage is based on 42"-wide fabric. Fat quarters measure 18" × 21".

3 yards of light solid for blocks
15 fat quarters of assorted prints for blocks
½ yard of aqua print for inner border
⅜ yard of gray floral for middle border
2 yards of red floral for outer border and binding
5¼ yards of fabric for backing
72" × 85" piece of batting

Cutting

All measurements include ¼"-wide seam allowances.

From the light solid, cut:
15 strips, 3½" × 42"; crosscut into 160 squares,
   3½" × 3½"
30 strips, 1½" × 42"; crosscut into 60 strips, 1½" × 21"

From *each* print fat quarter, cut:
1 strip, 6" × 21"; crosscut into:
   ◇ 1 square, 6" × 6"; cut into quarters diagonally to
      yield 4 side triangles (60 total; 10 will be extra)
   ◇ 3 squares, 3½" × 3½" (45 total; 1 will be extra)
5 strips, 1½" × 21" (75 total)

From *each of 4* print fat quarters, cut:
1 square, 4" × 4"; cut in half diagonally to yield 2 corner
   triangles (8 total; 1 of each print will be extra)

From the aqua print, cut:
7 strips, 2" × 42"

From the gray floral, cut:
7 strips, 1¼" × 42"

From the red floral, cut:
8 strips, 5½" × 42"
8 strips, 2¼" × 42"

Making the A and B Blocks

Press all seam allowances as indicated by the arrows.

1. Join two print and one light 1½"-wide strip along their long edges to make a strip set. Make *15 sets of two* matching strip sets (30 total). Cut each strip set into eight 1½"-wide segments.

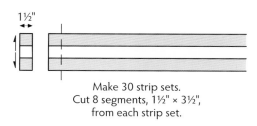

1½"

Make 30 strip sets.
Cut 8 segments, 1½" × 3½",
from each strip set.

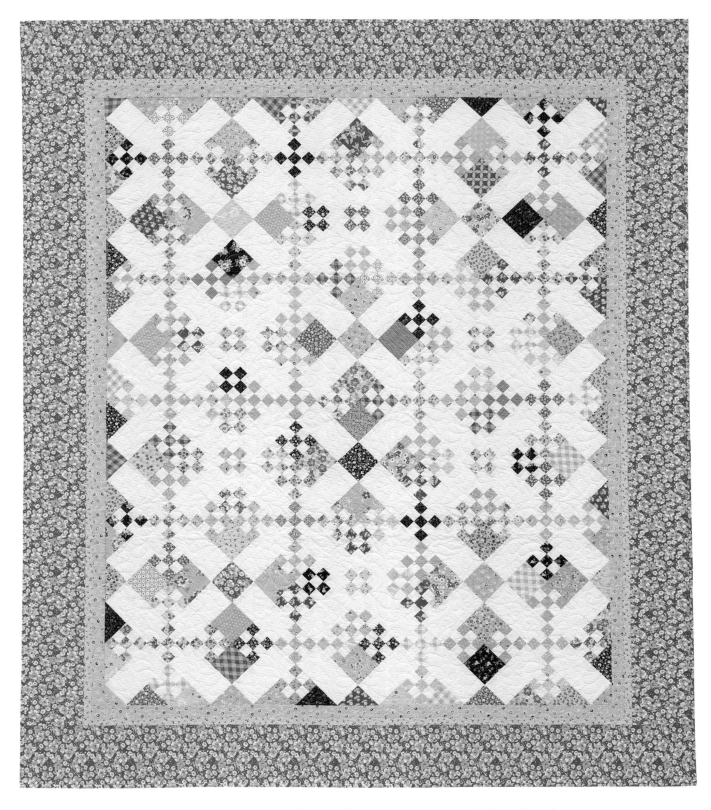

FINISHED QUILT: 66" × 78⅝" ∼ **FINISHED BLOCK:** 9" × 9"
Pieced by Doug Leko and Janet Moser; quilted by Sandy Pluff

2 Join two light and one print 1½"-wide strip along their long edges to make a strip set. Make 15 strip sets. Cut each strip set into 11 segments, 1½" wide.

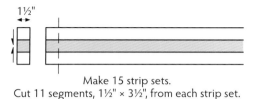

Make 15 strip sets.
Cut 11 segments, 1½" × 3½", from each strip set.

3 Using segments from the same print, lay out two segments from step 1 and one segment from step 2 as shown. Join the segments to make one A unit measuring 3½" square. Make 105 units.

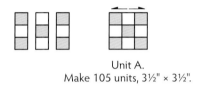

Unit A.
Make 105 units, 3½" × 3½".

4 Using segments from the same print, lay out one segment from step 1 and two segments from step 2 as shown. Join the segments to make one B unit measuring 3½" square. Make 30 units.

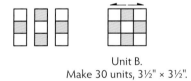

Unit B.
Make 30 units, 3½" × 3½".

5 Lay out five A units and four light 3½" squares in three rows. Sew the pieces together into rows. Join the rows to complete one of block A measuring 9½" square. Make 20 blocks. (You'll have five A units left over for another project.)

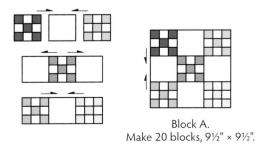

Block A.
Make 20 blocks, 9½" × 9½".

6 Lay out five B units and four light 3½" squares in three rows. Sew the pieces together into rows. Join the rows to complete one of block B measuring 9½" square. Make six blocks.

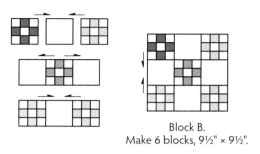

Block B.
Make 6 blocks, 9½" × 9½".

Making the C Blocks

Lay out five print and four light 3½" squares in three rows as shown. Sew the squares together into rows. Join the rows to complete one of block C measuring 9½" square. Make six blocks.

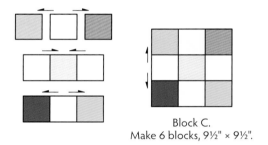

Block C.
Make 6 blocks, 9½" × 9½".

Making the Side and Corner Blocks

1 Lay out one print square, two light squares, and three print side triangles in three rows as shown. Join the pieces in the top and middle rows. Sew the rows together. Add the triangle to the bottom of the unit to complete a side block. Make 14 blocks.

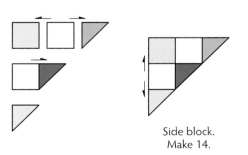

Side block.
Make 14.

2 Sew one light square and two print side triangles together. Add a print corner triangle to the bottom of the unit to complete one corner block. Make four blocks.

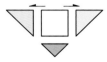

Corner block.
Make 4.

Assembling the Quilt Top

1 Lay out the A, B, and C blocks in diagonal rows as shown in the quilt assembly diagram at right. Add the side and corner blocks. Stitch the blocks together into diagonal rows. Join the rows, adding the corner blocks last. The triangles are cut slightly oversized for easier cutting and piecing. Trim and square up the quilt top, making sure to leave ¼" beyond the points of all the blocks for seam allowances. The quilt-top center should measure 51½" × 64⅛".

2 Join the aqua 2"-wide strips end to end using diagonal seams. From the pieced strip, cut two 64⅛"-long strips and two 54½"-long strips. Sew the 64⅛"-long strips to opposite sides of the quilt top. Sew the 54½"-long strips to the top and bottom of the quilt to complete the inner border. The quilt should measure 54½" × 67⅛", including the seam allowances.

3 Join the gray floral 1¼"-wide strips end to end using diagonal seams. From the pieced strip, cut two 67⅛"-long strips and two 56"-long strips. Sew the 67⅛"-long strips to opposite sides of the quilt top. Sew the 56"-long strips to the top and bottom of the quilt to complete the middle border. The quilt should measure 56" × 68⅝", including the seam allowances.

4 Join the red floral 5½"-wide strips end to end using diagonal seams. From the pieced strip, cut two 68⅝"-long strips and two 66"-long strips. Sew the 68⅝"-long strips to opposite sides of the quilt top. Sew the 66"-long strips to the top and bottom of the quilt to complete the outer border.

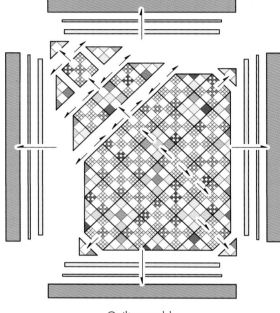

Quilt assembly

Finishing

For more details on any of the following steps, go to ShopMartingale.com/HowtoQuilt for free downloadable information.

1 Layer the quilt top with batting and backing. Baste the layers together.

2 Hand or machine quilt. The quilt shown is quilted with an overall swirl and feather design. Trim the batting and backing so the edges are even with the quilt top.

3 Use the red floral 2¼"-wide strips to make the binding, and then attach it to the quilt.

Alternate Colorway

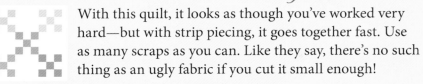

With this quilt, it looks as though you've worked very hard—but with strip piecing, it goes together fast. Use as many scraps as you can. Like they say, there's no such thing as an ugly fabric if you cut it small enough!

Pieced by Doug Leko and Janet Moser; quilted by Sandy Pluff

Rickrack Repeat

Start with strips for this fun design. The pieced triangles are cut from simple strip sets, which allows you to complete the blocks in no time.

Materials

Yardage is based on 42"-wide fabric. Fat quarters measure 18" × 21".

1½ yards of light print for blocks and inner border
16 fat quarters of assorted prints for blocks
¼ yard of black print for middle border
1¼ yards of purple print for outer border
½ yard of red print for binding
3⅞ yards of fabric for backing
62" × 76" piece of batting
Template plastic or 60° ruler

Cutting

All measurements include ¼"-wide seam allowances. Before you begin cutting, trace patterns A and B on page 76 onto template plastic and cut them out. Use the templates to cut the A and B pieces from the fabrics indicated below. If using a 60° ruler, you don't need to make an A template (see "Using a Ruler" on page 75).

From the light print, cut:
8 strips, 4½" × 42"; crosscut into:
  ◊ 2 rectangles, 4½" × 14⅜"
  ◊ 40 triangles using template A
  ◊ 40 triangles using template B
  ◊ 40 triangles using template B reversed
6 strips, 1½" × 42"

From *each* print fat quarter, cut:
7 strips, 1½" × 21" (112 total; 4 will be extra)

From the black print, cut:
6 strips, 1¼" × 42"

From the purple print, cut:
7 strips, 5½" × 42"

From the red print, cut:
7 strips, 2¼" × 42"

Making the Blocks

Press all seam allowances as indicated by the arrows.

1. Join four print 1½"-wide strips along their long edges to make a strip set. The strip set should measure 4½" × 21". Make 27 strip sets.

Make 27 strip sets,
4½" × 21".

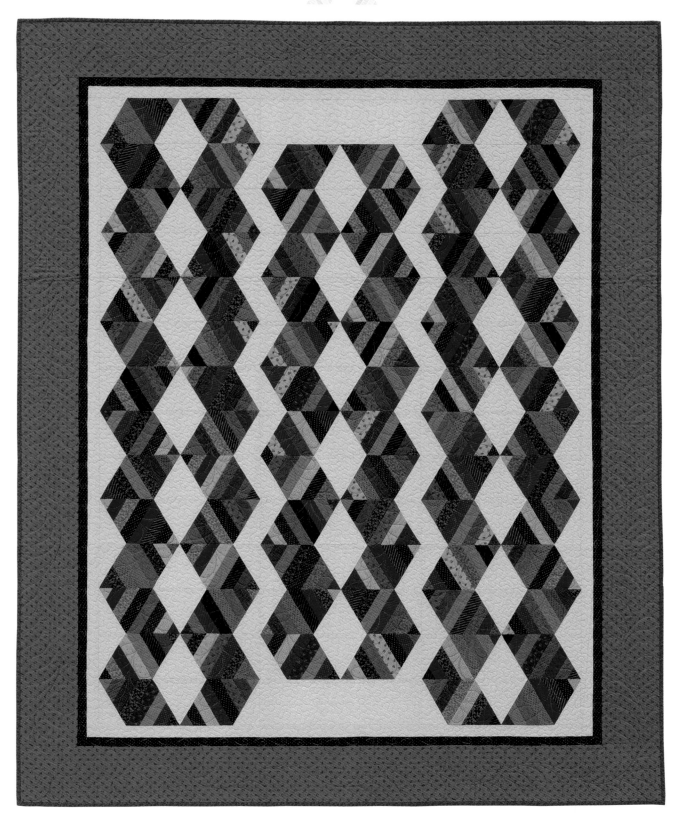

FINISHED QUILT: 55⅝" × 70" ~ **FINISHED BLOCK:** 4" × 13⅞"
Pieced by Doug Leko; quilted by Sandy Pluff

2 Use template A (or a 60° ruler) to cut six triangles from each strip set as shown. Cut a total of 162 triangles; two will be extra.

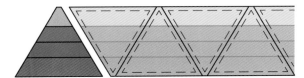

Cut 6 triangles from each strip set.

Using a Ruler

Instead of using a template, I use a 60° ruler from Creative Grids. When using a ruler, align the blunt tip and the 4½" line with the raw edges of the strip set.

3 Join two triangle units from step 2 as shown to make a diamond unit. Make 80 units.

Make 80.

4 Join a light reversed B triangle and one diamond unit as shown. Make 40 units.

 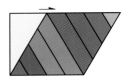

Make 40.

5 Repeat step 4 using the light B triangles and remaining diamond units to make 40 units.

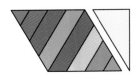 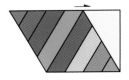

Make 40.

6 Lay out one light A triangle and one unit each from steps 4 and 5 as shown. Join the units to complete one block measuring 4½" × 14⅜". Make 40 blocks.

Make 40 blocks, 4½" × 14⅜".

Assembling the Quilt Top

1 Lay out the blocks and light rectangles in three vertical rows as shown in the quilt assembly diagram below. Stitch the blocks and rectangles together into rows. Join the rows to complete the quilt-top center. The quilt top should measure 42⅛" × 56½".

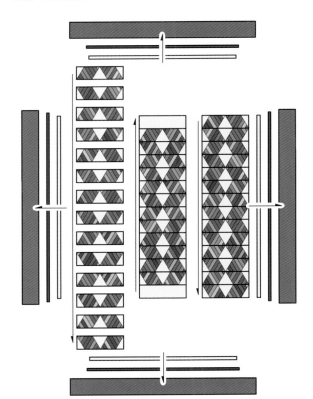

Quilt assembly

75

2 Join the light 1½"-wide strips end to end using diagonal seams. From the pieced strip, cut two 56½"-long strips and two 44⅛"-long strips. Sew the 56½"-long strips to opposite sides of the quilt top. Sew the 44⅛"-long strips to the top and bottom of the quilt to complete the inner border. The quilt should measure 44⅛" × 58½", including the seam allowances.

3 Join the black 1¼"-wide strips end to end using diagonal seams. From the pieced strip, cut two 58½"-long strips and two 45⅝"-long strips. Sew the 58½"-long strips to opposite sides of the quilt top. Sew the 45⅝"-long strips to the top and bottom of the quilt to complete the middle border. The quilt should measure 45⅝" × 60", including the seam allowances.

4 Join the purple 5½"-wide strips end to end using diagonal seams. From the pieced strip, cut two 60"-long strips and two 55⅝"-long strips. Sew the 60"-long strips to opposite sides of the quilt top. Sew the 55⅝"-long strips to the top and bottom of the quilt to complete the outer border.

Finishing

For more details on any of the following steps, go to ShopMartingale.com/HowtoQuilt for free downloadable information.

1 Layer the quilt top with batting and backing. Baste the layers together.

2 Hand or machine quilt. The quilt shown is quilted with a large feather design, plus stippling in the background. Trim the batting and backing so the edges are even with the quilt top.

3 Use the red 2¼"-wide strips to make the binding, and then attach it to the quilt.

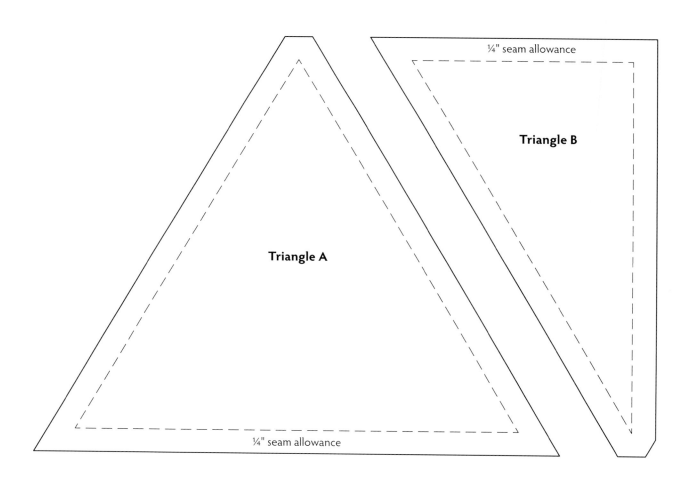

¼" seam allowance

Triangle B

Triangle A

¼" seam allowance

Alternate Colorway

For this colorway of Rickrack Repeat, I combined lots of small-, medium-, and large-scale prints in a bright mix of colors. To make your outer border and binding from the same fabric, you'll need to purchase 1¾ yards.

Pieced by Janet Moser; quilted by Sandy Pluff

Favorite Techniques

In this section, I share my favorite quiltmaking shortcuts. If you need more guidance on other aspects of quiltmaking, you'll find free, downloadable information on a variety of quiltmaking techniques on Martingale's website: ShopMartingale.com/HowtoQuilt. For my tips on using leftover fat quarters to make pieced backings, visit ShopMartingale.com/extras and look for *Stashtastic!*

Favorite Thread

I highly recommend Presencia 60-weight, 3-ply thread; it's thin, strong, durable, and produces virtually no lint. Check out my thread packs.

Flying-Geese Units

For each set of four matching flying-geese units, you'll need one large square and four matching small squares.

1 Place a ½"-wide ruler on the wrong side of a small square, aligning the centerline on the ruler on diagonally opposite corners of the square. Draw a line on each side of the ruler. Repeat to mark each small square.

2 With right sides together, place two marked squares on opposite corners of the large square. The points of the small squares will overlap just a bit and the drawn lines should extend across the large square from corner to corner as shown.

3 Stitch on both marked lines. Cut the units apart from corner to corner between the stitched lines. Press the seam allowances toward the small triangles.

Pressing Triangles

The seam on the small triangles is on the bias, so take extra care not to distort the triangles while pressing.

4 With right sides together, place the remaining marked squares on the corner of both units. Sew on the marked lines. Cut the units apart between the stitched lines to make four flying-geese units. Press the seam allowances toward

the small triangles. Trim each unit to the size specified in the project you are making.

Favorite Rulers

My preference for drawing lines for flying-geese and half-square-triangle units is the Omnigrid Marking Ruler Trio. For anything with a folded corner (such as a stitch-and-flip corner), I recommend my Simple Folded Corners Ruler.

Half-Square-Triangle Units

I make these units the easy way, using squares instead of triangles.

1 Cut two squares, one from each fabric, to the size specified in the cutting list.

2 Place a ½"-wide ruler on the wrong side of the lighter square, aligning the centerline on the ruler on diagonally opposite corners of the square. Draw a line on each side of the ruler.

3 Layer the two squares right sides together with the marked square on top. Stitch on both marked lines.

4 Cut the units apart from corner to corner between the stitched lines. Press the seam allowances toward the darker fabric unless instructed otherwise. Each pair of squares will yield two half-square-triangle units.

Spin the Seam Allowances

The following technique is useful when joining four fabric pieces or units to reduce bulk at the seam intersections.

1 Press three of the seam allowances so they're going in a clockwise direction. Notice that one seam allowance is not going in the same direction as the other three.

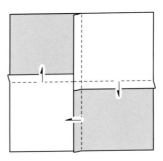

2 Flip back the fourth seam allowance so all of the seam allowances are going in a clockwise direction. The stitches above the crossed seam should pop apart, allowing the center of the unit to lie flat. If the stitches don't pop apart, use a seam ripper to help them along. If your seam allowances are pressed correctly, the center will look like a mini four-patch.

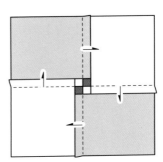

About the Author

Doug Leko founded Antler Quilt Design in 2008, when he was just 14 years old. He'd been quilting since the age of six, and working in his mother's quilt shop over the years helped him develop his skills and refine his art. After pattern testing for various designers, he began to develop his own quilt patterns. Doug took off from there, launching a full-scale design and marketing operation while he was still in high school and then throughout college.

Since then, his reputation has grown along with his business. Doug has a vibrant and expanding collection of patterns available at quilt stores around the world and online at AntlerQuiltDesign.com.

Doug takes a distinctive approach to his quilting designs. He enjoys incorporating secondary design elements into his quilt patterns, and he's absolutely passionate about color. For Doug, there's nothing like pulling together just the right mix of coordinating fabrics for a project. He loves every aspect of the quilting process, from design to fabric selection to handwork to binding.

Doug has released over 60 individual patterns, as well as nine self-published books. Each design is different from the next. His work has been featured in publications such as *McCall's Quilting, Quiltmaker,* and *American Patchwork & Quilting,* as well as many others. When he's not busy developing new designs or showing at Quilt Market, he divides his time between teaching and speaking at quilt shops and guilds and traveling the world.

Acknowledgments

A huge thank-you to the people that make what I do possible. Elaine (Mom), Mike (Dad), Janet, Marlene, and Sue—you are all so special to me and have influenced who I am today.

Thank you Moda Fabrics/United Notions for the fabrics used in this book. Many of the fabrics are from my Moda stash, and combined, they make up these wonderful quilts. Thanks also to the *many* people that work for this fantastic company that have made me feel a part of the family!

Thanks to Quilters Dream Batting for providing the best batting so my quilts will last a lifetime.

Presencia Thread, thank you for supplying me with a never-ending amount of the best threads.

Reliable Irons, I love my iron! When you have a great iron, your quilts look even better.